APR. 06

Test Results for Hardware Write Block Device: ICS ImageMasster DriveLock IDE (Firmware Version 17)

NCJ 212959

Glenn R. Schmitt
Acting Director

This report was prepared for the National Institute of Justice, U.S. Department of Justice, by the Office of Law Enforcement Standards of the National Institute of Standards and Technology under Interagency Agreement 2003–IJ–R–029.

The National Institute of Justice is a component of the Office of Justice Programs, which also includes the Bureau of Justice Assistance, the Bureau of Justice Statistics, the Office of Juvenile Justice and Delinquency Prevention, and the Office for Victims of Crime.

Test Results for Hardware Write Block Device:
ICS ImageMasster DriveLock IDE (Firmware Version 17)

April 2006

National Institute of Standards and Technology
Technology Administration, U.S. Department of Commerce

Contents

Introduction

The Computer Forensics Tool Testing (CFTT) program is a joint project of the National Institute of Justice (NIJ), the research and development organization of the U.S. Department of Justice, and the National Institute of Standards and Technology's (NIST's) Office of Law Enforcement Standards (OLES) and Information Technology Laboratory (ITL). CFTT is supported by other organizations, including the Federal Bureau of Investigation, the U.S. Department of Defense Cyber Crime Center, Internal Revenue Service Criminal Investigation's Electronic Crimes Program, and the U.S. Department of Homeland Security's Bureau of U.S. Immigration and Customs Enforcement and U.S. Secret Service. The objective of the CFTT program is to provide measurable assurance to practitioners, researchers, and other applicable users that the tools used in computer forensics investigations provide accurate results. Accomplishing this requires the development of specifications and test methods for computer forensics tools and subsequent testing of specific tools against those specifications.

Test results provide the information necessary for developers to improve tools, users to make informed choices, and the legal community and others to understand the tools' capabilities. This approach to testing computer forensic tools is based on well-recognized methodologies for conformance and quality testing. The specifications and test methods are posted on the CFTT Web site (http://www.cftt.nist.gov/) for review and comment by the computer forensics community.

This document reports the results from testing the ICS ImageMasster Drive Lock (Firmware Version 17) against *Hardware Write Blocker (HWB) Assertions and Test Plan Version 1.0*, which is available on the CFTT Web site (http://www.cftt.nist.gov/HWB-ATP-19.pdf). This specification identifies the following top-level tool requirements:

- A hardware write block (HWB) device shall not transmit a command to a protected storage device that modifies the data on the storage device.

- An HWB device shall return the data requested by a read operation.

- An HWB device shall return without modification any access-significant information requested from the drive.

- Any error condition reported by the storage device to the HWB device shall be reported to the host.

Test results from other software packages and the CFTT test methodology can be found on NIJ's computer forensics tool testing Web page (http://www.ojp.usdoj.gov/nij/topics/ecrime/cftt.htm).

Test Results for Hardware Write Block Devices

Device Tested: ICS ImageMasster DriveLock IDE (Firmware Version 17)

Input Interface: IDE (ATA)
Output Interface: IDE (ATA)

Supplier: Intelligent Computer Solutions, Inc.

Address: 9350 Eton Avenue
Chatsworth, CA 91311

Toll-free: 888–994–4678
Phone: 818–998–5805
Fax: 818–998–3190
E-mail: ics@ics-iq.com
http://www.ics-iq.com/

1   Results Summary by Requirements

An HWB device shall not transmit a command to a protected storage device that modifies the data on the storage device.
For all test cases run, the HWB device always blocked any commands that would have changed user or operating system data stored on a protected drive.

An HWB device shall return the data requested by a read operation.
For all test cases run, the HWB device always allowed commands to read the protected drive.

An HWB device shall return without modification any access-significant information requested from the drive.
For all test cases run, the HWB device always returned access-significant information from the protected drive without modification.

Any error condition reported by the storage device to the HWB device shall be reported to the host.
For all test cases run, the HWB device always returned error codes from the protected drive without modification.

2   Observations

- Although no commands were allowed by the write blocker that could change user or operating system data, some unsupported or atypical commands were allowed. Some examples are:

Command	Comment
Format Track (0x50)	This command is not defined in the current ATA hard drive specifications (ATA-4 through ATA-7). The command was defined in ATA-1, ATA-2, and ATA-3; however, all three specifications have been withdrawn. The command could be used to erase information on an older drive that supports the instruction, but could not be used to change the content of any user or operating system data stored on a drive.
SMART write (0xB0,D6)	This command records information in a device maintenance log that is not part of the data area where data files and operating system data are stored.
Vendor-specific commands	These are undocumented commands specific to a given model of hard drive.
CFA Erase Erase (0xC0)	This command applies to Compact Flash devices, not hard drives.
SATA Write FPDMA (0x61)	This command is noted by the protocol analyzer, but is only valid for Serial ATA (SATA) devices.

- Specific commands allowed are identified in test cases 01-h, 01-m, 01-r, 01-w, and 01-x.

- For the commands that manipulate the Host Protected Area (HPA) of a drive, 0xF9 and 0x37, the volatile variant of the commands is allowed, but the non-volatile variant is blocked.

- The tool blocked the 0x0F command, but the next command (a **read** command) was changed from LBA to PIO mode. The 0x0F command is reserved and undefined.

The tested device blocked the following commands in test case HWB-01-m:

```
0E=Reserved
0F=Reserved
3C=WRITE VERIFY
B1=DEVICE CONFIGURATION RESTORE (C0)
B1=DEVICE CONFIGURATION SET (C3)
```

The tested device blocked the following commands in test case HWB-01-w:

```
30=WRITE W/ RETRY
31=WRITE W/O RETRY
32=WRITE/L W/ RETR
33=WRITE/L W/O RTR
34=WRITE SECTOR EXT
35=WRITE DMA EXT
36=WR DMA QUE EXT
39=WRITE MULTI EXT
3A=WRITE STREAM DMA
3B=WRITE STREAM PIO
C5=WRITE MULTIPLE
CA=Write DMA
CB=WRT DMA W/O RTR
CC=WRITE DMA QUEUE
```

```
E7=FLUSH CACHE
E9=WRITE SAME
EA=FLUSH CACHE EXT
F3=SECUR ERASE PRE
F4=SECUR ERASE UNI
```

The tested device blocked the following commands in test case HWB-01-x:

```
F1=SECUR SET PASSW
92=DOWNLD MICROCOD
```

The tested device blocked the following commands in test case HWB-01-h:

```
37=SET MAX ADR EXT (non-volatile)
F9=SET MAX ADDRESS (non-volatile)
```

3 Test Case Selection

Since a protocol analyzer was available, the following test cases are appropriate: HWB-01, HWB-03, HWB-06, HWB-08, and HWB-09.

For test case HWB-01, the command set was divided into five sets of commands: 01-r (read), 01-w (write), 01-x (potential to damage a drive), 01-h (host protected area), and 01-m (everything else).

For test case HWB-03, two variations were selected: boot (attempt to boot from a protected drive) and image (use an imaging tool to attempt to write to a protected drive).

For test case HWB-06, two variations were selected: en (use a DOS-based imaging tool [EnCase] to read from a protected drive) and ix (use a stand-alone imaging tool [IXimager] to read from a protected drive).

4 Testing Environment

The tests were run in the NIST CFTT lab. This section describes the hardware (test computers and hard drives) available for testing. Not all components were used in testing; for example, the ZIP drive on Beta-5 was not used.

4.1 Test Computers

The test computer for all test cases except 03-boot was **Freddy:**

Intel Desktop Motherboard D865GB/D865PERC (with ATA-6 IDE onboard controller)
BIOS Version BF86510A.86A.0053.P13
Adaptec SCSI BIOS V3.10.0
Intel Pentium® 4 CPU
SONY DVD RW DRU–530A, ATAPI CD/DVD–ROM drive
1.44MB floppy drive
Two slots for removable IDE hard disk drives
Two slots for removable SATA hard disk drives

Two slots for removable SCSI hard disk drive

Beta-5 was used for only one test case, 03-boot. Beta-5 is a Dell Computer Corporation system with 256MB RAM, one hard disk drive bay, one installed 15.37GB hard disk, a CD–ROM drive, a 1.44MB floppy drive, and a 250MB ZIP drive. The BIOS is PhoenixBios 4.0 Release 6.0.

4.2 Protocol Analyzer

A Data Transit bus protocol analyzer (Bus Doctor Rx) was used to monitor and record commands sent from the host to the write blocker and from the write blocker to the protected hard drive. Two identical protocol analyzers were available for monitoring commands.

One of two Dell laptop computers (either Chip or Dale) was connected to each protocol analyzer to record commands observed by the protocol analyzer.

4.3 Hard Disk Drives

The hard disk drives that were used were selected from the drives listed below. These hard drives were mounted in removable storage modules. The drives are set up in a variety of ways with the common partition types (FAT and NTFS) represented. The setup of each drive is documented below.

```
Drive label: 7c
Partition table Drive /dev/hdc
04865/254/63 (max cyl/hd values)
04866/255/63 (number of cyl/hd)
78177792 total number of sectors
IDE disk: Model (MAXTOR 6L040J2) serial # (662201137769)
 N    Start LBA Length    Start C/H/S End C/H/S    boot Partition type
 1 P 000000063 078156162 0000/001/01 1023/254/63 Boot 07 NTFS
 2 P 000000000 000000000 0000/000/00 0000/000/00      00 empty entry
 3 P 000000000 000000000 0000/000/00 0000/000/00      00 empty entry
 4 P 000000000 000000000 0000/000/00 0000/000/00      00 empty entry
Drive label: 74
Partition table Drive /dev/hdc
05004/254/63 (max cyl/hd values)
05005/255/63 (number of cyl/hd)
80418240 total number of sectors
IDE disk: Model (IC35L040AVER07-0) serial # (SXPTXHQ6113)
 N    Start LBA Length    Start C/H/S End C/H/S    boot Partition type
 1 P 000000063 080405262 0000/001/01 1023/254/63      0C Fat32X
 2 P 000000000 000000000 0000/000/00 0000/000/00      00 empty entry
 3 P 000000000 000000000 0000/000/00 0000/000/00      00 empty entry
 4 P 000000000 000000000 0000/000/00 0000/000/00      00 empty entry
Drive label: a8
Partition table Drive /dev/hdc
02433/254/63 (max cyl/hd values)
02434/255/63 (number of cyl/hd)
39102336 total number of sectors
IDE disk: Model (WDC WD200BB-00AUA1) serial # (WD-WMA6Y3401179)
 N    Start LBA Length    Start C/H/S End C/H/S    boot Partition type
 1 P 000000063 000016002 0000/001/01 0000/254/63      01 Fat12
 2 X 000016065 039086145 0001/000/01 1023/254/63      0F extended
 3 S 000000063 039086082 0001/001/01 1023/254/63      0B Fat32
 4 S 000000000 000000000 0000/000/00 0000/000/00      00 empty entry
 5 P 000000000 000000000 0000/000/00 0000/000/00      00 empty entry
```

```
  6 P 000000000 000000000 0000/000/00 0000/000/00        00 empty entry
Drive label: bf
Partition table Drive /dev/hdc
30400/254/63 (max cyl/hd values)
30401/255/63 (number of cyl/hd)
488397168 total number of sectors
IDE disk: Model (WDC WD2500JB-00GVA0) serial # (WD-WCAL73854148)
  N   Start LBA Length     Start C/H/S End C/H/S   boot Partition type
  1 P 000000063 409609242 0000/001/01 1023/254/63      0C Fat32X
  2 X 409609305 000016065 1023/000/01 1023/254/63      0F extended
  3 S 000000063 000016002 1023/001/01 1023/254/63      01 Fat12
  4 S 000000000 000000000 0000/000/00 0000/000/00      00 empty entry
  5 P 000000000 000000000 0000/000/00 0000/000/00      00 empty entry
  6 P 000000000 000000000 0000/000/00 0000/000/00      00 empty entry
```

Drive xx is used as it is and is not set up. This drive is used to test commands that do low-level changes to the drive.

P primary partition (1-4)
S secondary (sub) partition
X primary extended partition (1-4)
x secondary extended partition

4.4 Support Software

The software in the following table was used to send commands to the protected drive. Two widely used imaging tools, EnCase and IXimager, were used to generate disk activity (reads and writes) consistent with a realistic scenario of an accidental modification of an unprotected hard drive during a forensic examination. This does not imply an endorsement of the imaging tools.

Program	Description
ATASEND	A tool to send ATA commands to a drive.
FS–TST	Software from the FS–TST tools was used to generate errors from the hard drive by trying to read beyond the end of the drive. The FS–TST software was also used to set up the hard drives and print partition tables and drive size.
EnCase	An imaging tool (EnCase 3.22g, DOS) for test case 03-img.
IXimager	An imaging tool (ILook IXimager Version 1.0, August 25, 2004) for test case 03-img.

5 Interpretation of Test Results

The main item of interest for interpreting the test results is determining the device's conformance to the test assertions. This section lists each test assertion and identifies the information in the log files relevant to conformance with the assertion. Conformance of each assertion tested by a given test case is evaluated by examining the Blocker Input and Blocker Output boxes of the test report summary.

5.1 Test Results Report Key

A summary of the actual test results is presented in this report. The following table presents a description of each section of the test report summary.

Heading	Description
First Line	Test case ID, name and version of software tested.
Case Summary	Test case summary from *Hardware Write Blocker (HWB) Assertions and Test Plan Version 1.0.*
Assertions Tested	Test assertions tested by the test case from *Hardware Write Blocker (HWB) Assertions and Test Plan Version 1.0.*
Tester Name	Name or initials of person executing test procedure.
Test Date	Time and date that test was started.
Test Configuration	Identification of the following: 1. Label of the protected hard drive. 2. Interface between host and blocker. 3. Interface between blocker and protected drive. 4. Protocol analyzers monitoring each interface. 5. Laptop attached to each protocol analyzer. 6. Execution environment for tool sending commands from the host.
Hard Drives Used	Description of the protected hard drive.
Blocker Input	A list of commands sent from the host to the blocker. For test case HWB-01, a list of the command codes sent is provided, followed by a count of the commands sent. For test cases HWB-03 and HWB-06, a list of the commands sent and the number of times each command was sent.
Blocker Output	A list of commands observed by the protocol analyzer on the bus from the blocker to the protected drive. For test case HWB-01, a list of the command codes observed on the bus between the blocker and the protected drive is provided, followed by a count of the number of commands sent (from the Blocker Input box) and a count of the number of commands observed on the bus between the blocker and the protected drive. For test cases HWB-03 and HWB-06, a list of the commands sent and the number of times each command was sent.
Results	Expected and actual results for each assertion tested.
Analysis	Whether or not the expected results were achieved.

5.2 Test Details

Test Case HWB-01 Variation 01-h ICS ImageMasster DriveLock IDE FW v17	
Case Summary:	HWB-01 Identify commands blocked by the HWB.
Assertions Tested:	HWB-AM-01 The HWB shall not transmit any modifying category operation to the protected storage device. HWB-AM-05 The action that an HWB device takes for any commands not assigned to the modifying, read, or information categories is defined by the vendor.
Tester Name:	kbr
Test Date:	run start Mon Aug 29 11:42:46 2005 run finish Mon Aug 29 11:44:17 2005
Test Configuration:	HOST: freddy HostToBlocker Monitor: dale HostToBlocker PA: aa00155 HostToBlocker Interface: IDE BlockerToDrive Monitor: chip BlockerToDrive PA: aa00111 BlockerToDrive Interface: IDE Run Environment: DOS
Drives:	Protected drive: bf bf is a WDC WD2500JB-00GVA0 serial # WD-WCAL73854148 with 488397168 sectors
Blocker Input:	Commands Sent to Blocker
Blocker Output:	Commands Allowed by Blocker

Blocker Input: Commands Sent to Blocker

Command	LBA/CHS
F8=RD NATV MAX ADD	LBA=0000000
F9=SET MAX ADDRESS	LBA=8000000
F8=RD NATV MAX ADD	LBA=0000000
F9=SET MAX ADDRESS	LBA=8000000
27=RD MAX ADR EXT	LBA=000000000000
37=SET MAX ADR EXT	LBA=000000000000
27=RD MAX ADR EXT	LBA=000000000000
37=SET MAX ADR EXT	LBA=000000000000

8 commands sent

Blocker Output: Commands Allowed by Blocker

Command	LBA/CHS
F8=RD NATV MAX ADD	LBA=0000000
F8=RD NATV MAX ADD	LBA=0000000
F9=SET MAX ADDRESS	LBA=8000000
27=RD MAX ADR EXT	LBA=000000000000
27=RD MAX ADR EXT	LBA=000000000000
37=SET MAX ADR EXT	LBA=000000000000

	8 commands sent, 6 commands allowed
Results:	
		Assertion	Expected Result	Actual Result
	|---|---|---
		AM-01	Modifying commands blocked	Modifying commands blocked
		AM-05	HWB behavior recorded	HWB behavior recorded
Analysis:	Expected results achieved

Test Case HWB-01 Variation 01-m ICS ImageMasster DriveLock IDE FW v17	
Case Summary:	HWB-01 Identify commands blocked by the HWB.
Assertions Tested:	HWB-AM-01 The HWB shall not transmit any modifying category operation to the protected storage device. HWB-AM-05 The action that an HWB device takes for any commands not assigned to the modifying, read, or information categories is defined by the vendor.
Tester Name:	kbr
Test Date:	run start Mon Aug 29 11:27:54 2005 run finish Mon Aug 29 11:41:20 2005
Test Configuration:	HOST: freddy HostToBlocker Monitor: dale HostToBlocker PA: aa00155 HostToBlocker Interface: IDE BlockerToDrive Monitor: chip BlockerToDrive PA: aa00111 BlockerToDrive Interface: IDE Run Environment: DOS
Drives:	Protected drive: bf bf is a WDC WD2500JB-00GVA0 serial # WD-WCAL73854148 with 488397168 sectors
Blocker Input:	Commands Sent to Blocker

Command	LBA/CHS
00=NOP	Cyl: 0000, Head: 0, Sec: 00
01=Reserved	Cyl: 0000, Head: 0, Sec: 00
02=Reserved	Cyl: 0000, Head: 0, Sec: 00
03=CFA REQ ERR CODE	Cyl: 0000, Head: 0, Sec: 00
04=Reserved	Cyl: 0000, Head: 0, Sec: 00
05=Reserved	Cyl: 0000, Head: 0, Sec: 00
06=Reserved	Cyl: 0000, Head: 0, Sec: 00
07=Reserved	Cyl: 0000, Head: 0, Sec: 00
08=DEVICE RESET	Cyl: 0000, Head: 0, Sec: 00
09=Reserved	Cyl: 0000, Head: 0, Sec: 00

0A=Reserved	Cyl: 0000, Head: 0, Sec: 00	
0B=Reserved	Cyl: 0000, Head: 0, Sec: 00	
0C=Reserved	Cyl: 0000, Head: 0, Sec: 00	
0D=Reserved	Cyl: 0000, Head: 0, Sec: 00	
0E=Reserved	Cyl: 0000, Head: 0, Sec: 00	
0F=Reserved	Cyl: 0000, Head: 0, Sec: 00	
10=RECALIBRATE	Cyl: 0000, Head: 0, Sec: 00	
11=RECALIBRATE	Cyl: 0000, Head: 0, Sec: 00	
12=RECALIBRATE	Cyl: 0000, Head: 0, Sec: 00	
13=RECALIBRATE	Cyl: 0000, Head: 0, Sec: 00	
14=RECALIBRATE	Cyl: 0000, Head: 0, Sec: 00	
15=RECALIBRATE	Cyl: 0000, Head: 0, Sec: 00	
16=RECALIBRATE	Cyl: 0000, Head: 0, Sec: 00	
17=RECALIBRATE	Cyl: 0000, Head: 0, Sec: 00	
18=RECALIBRATE	Cyl: 0000, Head: 0, Sec: 00	
19=RECALIBRATE	Cyl: 0000, Head: 0, Sec: 00	
1A=RECALIBRATE	Cyl: 0000, Head: 0, Sec: 00	
1B=RECALIBRATE	Cyl: 0000, Head: 0, Sec: 00	
1C=RECALIBRATE	Cyl: 0000, Head: 0, Sec: 00	
1D=RECALIBRATE	Cyl: 0000, Head: 0, Sec: 00	
1E=RECALIBRATE	Cyl: 0000, Head: 0, Sec: 00	
1F=RECALIBRATE	Cyl: 0000, Head: 0, Sec: 00	
28=Reserved	Cyl: 0000, Head: 0, Sec: 00	
2C=Reserved	Cyl: 0000, Head: 0, Sec: 00	
2D=Reserved	Cyl: 0000, Head: 0, Sec: 00	
2E=Reserved	Cyl: 0000, Head: 0, Sec: 00	
3C=WRITE VERIFY	Cyl: 0000, Head: 0, Sec: 00	
43=Reserved	Cyl: 0000, Head: 0, Sec: 00	
44=Reserved	Cyl: 0000, Head: 0, Sec: 00	
45=Reserved	Cyl: 0000, Head: 0, Sec: 00	
46=Reserved	Cyl: 0000, Head: 0, Sec: 00	
47=Reserved	Cyl: 0000, Head: 0, Sec: 00	
48=Reserved	Cyl: 0000, Head: 0, Sec: 00	
49=Reserved	Cyl: 0000, Head: 0, Sec: 00	
4A=Reserved	Cyl: 0000, Head: 0, Sec: 00	
4B=Reserved	Cyl: 0000, Head: 0, Sec: 00	
4C=Reserved	Cyl: 0000, Head: 0, Sec: 00	
4D=Reserved	Cyl: 0000, Head: 0, Sec: 00	
4E=Reserved	Cyl: 0000, Head: 0, Sec: 00	
4F=Reserved	Cyl: 0000, Head: 0, Sec: 00	
51=CONFIG STREAM	LBA=000000000000	
52=Reserved	Cyl: 0000, Head: 0, Sec: 00	
53=Reserved	Cyl: 0000, Head: 0, Sec: 00	
54=Reserved	Cyl: 0000, Head: 0, Sec: 00	
55=Reserved	Cyl: 0000, Head: 0, Sec: 00	
56=Reserved	Cyl: 0000, Head: 0, Sec: 00	

57=Reserved	Cyl: 0000, Head: 0, Sec: 00	
58=Reserved	Cyl: 0000, Head: 0, Sec: 00	
59=Reserved	Cyl: 0000, Head: 0, Sec: 00	
5A=Reserved	Cyl: 0000, Head: 0, Sec: 00	
5B=Reserved	Cyl: 0000, Head: 0, Sec: 00	
5C=Reserved	Cyl: 0000, Head: 0, Sec: 00	
5D=Reserved	Cyl: 0000, Head: 0, Sec: 00	
5E=Reserved	Cyl: 0000, Head: 0, Sec: 00	
5F=Reserved	Cyl: 0000, Head: 0, Sec: 00	
60=Read FPDMA Queued	Cyl: 0000, Head: 0, Sec: 00	
61=Write FPDMA Queued	Cyl: 0000, Head: 0, Sec: 00	
62=Reserved	Cyl: 0000, Head: 0, Sec: 00	
63=Reserved	Cyl: 0000, Head: 0, Sec: 00	
64=Reserved	Cyl: 0000, Head: 0, Sec: 00	
65=Reserved	Cyl: 0000, Head: 0, Sec: 00	
66=Reserved	Cyl: 0000, Head: 0, Sec: 00	
67=SEP_ATTN	Cyl: 0000, Head: 0, Sec: 00	
68=Reserved	Cyl: 0000, Head: 0, Sec: 00	
69=Reserved	Cyl: 0000, Head: 0, Sec: 00	
6A=Reserved	Cyl: 0000, Head: 0, Sec: 00	
6B=Reserved	Cyl: 0000, Head: 0, Sec: 00	
6C=Reserved	Cyl: 0000, Head: 0, Sec: 00	
6D=Reserved	Cyl: 0000, Head: 0, Sec: 00	
6E=Reserved	Cyl: 0000, Head: 0, Sec: 00	
6F=Reserved	Cyl: 0000, Head: 0, Sec: 00	
70=SEEK	Cyl: 0000, Head: 0, Sec: 00	
71=SEEK	Cyl: 0000, Head: 0, Sec: 00	
72=SEEK	Cyl: 0000, Head: 0, Sec: 00	
73=SEEK	Cyl: 0000, Head: 0, Sec: 00	
74=SEEK	Cyl: 0000, Head: 0, Sec: 00	
75=SEEK	Cyl: 0000, Head: 0, Sec: 00	
76=SEEK	Cyl: 0000, Head: 0, Sec: 00	
77=SEEK	Cyl: 0000, Head: 0, Sec: 00	
78=SEEK	Cyl: 0000, Head: 0, Sec: 00	
79=SEEK	Cyl: 0000, Head: 0, Sec: 00	
7A=SEEK	Cyl: 0000, Head: 0, Sec: 00	
7B=SEEK	Cyl: 0000, Head: 0, Sec: 00	
7C=SEEK	Cyl: 0000, Head: 0, Sec: 00	
7D=SEEK	Cyl: 0000, Head: 0, Sec: 00	
7E=SEEK	Cyl: 0000, Head: 0, Sec: 00	
7F=SEEK	Cyl: 0000, Head: 0, Sec: 00	
80=Reserved	Cyl: 0000, Head: 0, Sec: 00	
81=Reserved	Cyl: 0000, Head: 0, Sec: 00	
82=Reserved	Cyl: 0000, Head: 0, Sec: 00	
83=Reserved	Cyl: 0000, Head: 0, Sec: 00	
84=Reserved	Cyl: 0000, Head: 0, Sec: 00	

85=Reserved	Cyl: 0000, Head: 0, Sec: 00
86=Reserved	Cyl: 0000, Head: 0, Sec: 00
87=CFA TRNSLT SCTR	LBA=0000000
88=Reserved	Cyl: 0000, Head: 0, Sec: 00
89=Reserved	Cyl: 0000, Head: 0, Sec: 00
8A=Reserved	Cyl: 0000, Head: 0, Sec: 00
8B=Reserved	Cyl: 0000, Head: 0, Sec: 00
8C=Reserved	Cyl: 0000, Head: 0, Sec: 00
8D=Reserved	Cyl: 0000, Head: 0, Sec: 00
8E=Reserved	Cyl: 0000, Head: 0, Sec: 00
8F=Reserved	Cyl: 0000, Head: 0, Sec: 00
90=EXEC DRIVE DIAG	Cyl: 0000, Head: 0, Sec: 00
93=Reserved	Cyl: 0000, Head: 0, Sec: 00
94=STANDBY IMMEDIA	Cyl: 0000, Head: 0, Sec: 00
95=IDLE IMMEDIATE	Cyl: 0000, Head: 0, Sec: 00
96=STANDBY	Cyl: 0000, Head: 0, Sec: 00
97=IDLE	Cyl: 0000, Head: 0, Sec: 00
98=CHECK POWER MOD	Cyl: 0000, Head: 0, Sec: 00
99=SLEEP	Cyl: 0000, Head: 0, Sec: 00
9A=Reserved	Cyl: 0000, Head: 0, Sec: 00
9B=Reserved	Cyl: 0000, Head: 0, Sec: 00
9C=Reserved	Cyl: 0000, Head: 0, Sec: 00
9D=Reserved	Cyl: 0000, Head: 0, Sec: 00
9E=Reserved	Cyl: 0000, Head: 0, Sec: 00
9F=Reserved	Cyl: 0000, Head: 0, Sec: 00
A1=ATAPI ID DRIVE	Cyl: 0000, Head: 0, Sec: 00
A2=ATAPI SERVICE	Cyl: 0000, Head: 0, Sec: 00
A3=Reserved	Cyl: 0000, Head: 0, Sec: 00
A4=Reserved	Cyl: 0000, Head: 0, Sec: 00
A5=Reserved	Cyl: 0000, Head: 0, Sec: 00
A6=Reserved	Cyl: 0000, Head: 0, Sec: 00
A7=Reserved	Cyl: 0000, Head: 0, Sec: 00
A8=Reserved	Cyl: 0000, Head: 0, Sec: 00
A9=Reserved	Cyl: 0000, Head: 0, Sec: 00
AA=Reserved	Cyl: 0000, Head: 0, Sec: 00
AB=Reserved	Cyl: 0000, Head: 0, Sec: 00
AC=Reserved	Cyl: 0000, Head: 0, Sec: 00
AD=Reserved	Cyl: 0000, Head: 0, Sec: 00
AE=Reserved	Cyl: 0000, Head: 0, Sec: 00
AF=Reserved	Cyl: 0000, Head: 0, Sec: 00
B0=SMART D9=Smart Disable Operation	Cyl: 0000, Head: 0, Sec: 00
B0=SMART DA=Smart Return Stats	Cyl: 0000, Head: 0, Sec: 00
B0=SMART D2=Smart Enable/Disable AT	Cyl: 0000, Head: 0, Sec: 00

B0=SMART D8=Smart Enable Operation	Cyl: 0000, Head: 0, Sec: 00	
B0=SMART D4=Smart Execute Offline	Cyl: 0000, Head: 0, Sec: 00	
B1=Device Config	Cyl: 0000, Head: 0, Sec: 00	
B1=Device Config	Cyl: 0000, Head: 0, Sec: 00	
B1=Device Config	Cyl: 0000, Head: 0, Sec: 00	
B1=Device Config	Cyl: 0000, Head: 0, Sec: 00	
B2=Reserved	Cyl: 0000, Head: 0, Sec: 00	
B3=Reserved	Cyl: 0000, Head: 0, Sec: 00	
B4=Reserved	Cyl: 0000, Head: 0, Sec: 00	
B5=Reserved	Cyl: 0000, Head: 0, Sec: 00	
B6=Reserved	Cyl: 0000, Head: 0, Sec: 00	
B7=Reserved	Cyl: 0000, Head: 0, Sec: 00	
B8=Reserved	Cyl: 0000, Head: 0, Sec: 00	
B9=Reserved	Cyl: 0000, Head: 0, Sec: 00	
BA=Reserved	Cyl: 0000, Head: 0, Sec: 00	
BB=Reserved	Cyl: 0000, Head: 0, Sec: 00	
BC=Reserved	Cyl: 0000, Head: 0, Sec: 00	
BD=Reserved	Cyl: 0000, Head: 0, Sec: 00	
BE=Reserved	Cyl: 0000, Head: 0, Sec: 00	
BF=Reserved	Cyl: 0000, Head: 0, Sec: 00	
C1=Reserved	Cyl: 0000, Head: 0, Sec: 00	
C2=Reserved	Cyl: 0000, Head: 0, Sec: 00	
C3=Reserved	Cyl: 0000, Head: 0, Sec: 00	
C6=SET MULTPLE MOD	Cyl: 0000, Head: 0, Sec: 00	
CF=Reserved	Cyl: 0000, Head: 0, Sec: 00	
D0=Reserved	Cyl: 0000, Head: 0, Sec: 00	
D1=CHK MD Card Type	Cyl: 0000, Head: 0, Sec: 00	
D2=Reserved	Cyl: 0000, Head: 0, Sec: 00	
D3=Reserved	Cyl: 0000, Head: 0, Sec: 00	
D4=Reserved	Cyl: 0000, Head: 0, Sec: 00	
D5=Reserved	Cyl: 0000, Head: 0, Sec: 00	
D6=Reserved	Cyl: 0000, Head: 0, Sec: 00	
D7=Reserved	Cyl: 0000, Head: 0, Sec: 00	
D8=Reserved	Cyl: 0000, Head: 0, Sec: 00	
D9=Reserved	Cyl: 0000, Head: 0, Sec: 00	
DA=Get Media Sts	Cyl: 0000, Head: 0, Sec: 00	
DB=ACK MEDIA CHG	Cyl: 0000, Head: 0, Sec: 00	
DC=BOOT POST-BOOT	Cyl: 0000, Head: 0, Sec: 00	
DD=BOOT PRE-BOOT	Cyl: 0000, Head: 0, Sec: 00	
DE=MEDIA LOCK	Cyl: 0000, Head: 0, Sec: 00	
DF=MEDIA UNLOCK	Cyl: 0000, Head: 0, Sec: 00	
E0=STANDBY IMMEDIA	Cyl: 0000, Head: 0, Sec: 00	
E1=IDLE IMMEDIATE	Cyl: 0000, Head: 0, Sec: 00	
E2=STANDBY	Cyl: 0000, Head: 0, Sec: 00	

	E3=IDLE	Cyl: 0000, Head: 0, Sec: 00
	E5=CHECK POWER MOD	Cyl: 0000, Head: 0, Sec: 00
	E6=SLEEP	Cyl: 0000, Head: 0, Sec: 00
	EB=Reserved	Cyl: 0000, Head: 0, Sec: 00
	EC=IDENTIFY DRIVE	Cyl: 0000, Head: 0, Sec: 00
	ED=MEDIA EJECT	Cyl: 0000, Head: 0, Sec: 00
	EE=IDENT DEVICE DM	Cyl: 0000, Head: 0, Sec: 00
	EF=SET FEATURES 00=Unknown	Cyl: 0000, Head: 0, Sec: 00
	F0=Reserved	Cyl: 0000, Head: 0, Sec: 00
	F2=SECURITY UNLOCK	Cyl: 0000, Head: 0, Sec: 00
	F5=SECURITY FREEZE	Cyl: 0000, Head: 0, Sec: 00
	F6=SECUR DSABL PAS	Cyl: 0000, Head: 0, Sec: 00
	F7=Reserved	Cyl: 0000, Head: 0, Sec: 00
	FA=Reserved	Cyl: 0000, Head: 0, Sec: 00
	FB=Reserved	Cyl: 0000, Head: 0, Sec: 00
	FC=Reserved	Cyl: 0000, Head: 0, Sec: 00
	FD=Reserved	Cyl: 0000, Head: 0, Sec: 00
	FE=Reserved	Cyl: 0000, Head: 0, Sec: 00
	FF=Reserved	Cyl: 0000, Head: 0, Sec: 00

208 commands sent

Blocker Output:

Commands Allowed by Blocker

Command	LBA/CHS
00=NOP	Cyl: 0000, Head: 0, Sec: 00
01=Reserved	Cyl: 0000, Head: 0, Sec: 00
02=Reserved	Cyl: 0000, Head: 0, Sec: 00
03=CFA REQ ERR CODE	Cyl: 0000, Head: 0, Sec: 00
04=Reserved	Cyl: 0000, Head: 0, Sec: 00
05=Reserved	Cyl: 0000, Head: 0, Sec: 00
06=Reserved	Cyl: 0000, Head: 0, Sec: 00
07=Reserved	Cyl: 0000, Head: 0, Sec: 00
08=DEVICE RESET	Cyl: 0000, Head: 0, Sec: 00
09=Reserved	Cyl: 0000, Head: 0, Sec: 00
0A=Reserved	Cyl: 0000, Head: 0, Sec: 00
0B=Reserved	Cyl: 0000, Head: 0, Sec: 00
0C=Reserved	Cyl: 0000, Head: 0, Sec: 00
0D=Reserved	Cyl: 0000, Head: 0, Sec: 00
20=READ W/ RETRY	Cyl: 0000, Head: 0, Sec: 00
10=RECALIBRATE	Cyl: 0000, Head: 0, Sec: 00
11=RECALIBRATE	Cyl: 0000, Head: 0, Sec: 00
12=RECALIBRATE	Cyl: 0000, Head: 0, Sec: 00
13=RECALIBRATE	Cyl: 0000, Head: 0, Sec: 00
14=RECALIBRATE	Cyl: 0000, Head: 0, Sec: 00

	15=RECALIBRATE	Cyl: 0000, Head: 0, Sec: 00
	16=RECALIBRATE	Cyl: 0000, Head: 0, Sec: 00
	17=RECALIBRATE	Cyl: 0000, Head: 0, Sec: 00
	18=RECALIBRATE	Cyl: 0000, Head: 0, Sec: 00
	19=RECALIBRATE	Cyl: 0000, Head: 0, Sec: 00
	1A=RECALIBRATE	Cyl: 0000, Head: 0, Sec: 00
	1B=RECALIBRATE	Cyl: 0000, Head: 0, Sec: 00
	1C=RECALIBRATE	Cyl: 0000, Head: 0, Sec: 00
	1D=RECALIBRATE	Cyl: 0000, Head: 0, Sec: 00
	1E=RECALIBRATE	Cyl: 0000, Head: 0, Sec: 00
	1F=RECALIBRATE	Cyl: 0000, Head: 0, Sec: 00
	28=Reserved	Cyl: 0000, Head: 0, Sec: 00
	2C=Reserved	Cyl: 0000, Head: 0, Sec: 00
	2D=Reserved	Cyl: 0000, Head: 0, Sec: 00
	2E=Reserved	Cyl: 0000, Head: 0, Sec: 00
	43=Reserved	Cyl: 0000, Head: 0, Sec: 00
	44=Reserved	Cyl: 0000, Head: 0, Sec: 00
	45=Reserved	Cyl: 0000, Head: 0, Sec: 00
	46=Reserved	Cyl: 0000, Head: 0, Sec: 00
	47=Reserved	Cyl: 0000, Head: 0, Sec: 00
	48=Reserved	Cyl: 0000, Head: 0, Sec: 00
	49=Reserved	Cyl: 0000, Head: 0, Sec: 00
	4A=Reserved	Cyl: 0000, Head: 0, Sec: 00
	4B=Reserved	Cyl: 0000, Head: 0, Sec: 00
	4C=Reserved	Cyl: 0000, Head: 0, Sec: 00
	4D=Reserved	Cyl: 0000, Head: 0, Sec: 00
	4E=Reserved	Cyl: 0000, Head: 0, Sec: 00
	4F=Reserved	Cyl: 0000, Head: 0, Sec: 00
	51=CONFIG STREAM	LBA=000000000000
	52=Reserved	Cyl: 0000, Head: 0, Sec: 00
	53=Reserved	Cyl: 0000, Head: 0, Sec: 00
	54=Reserved	Cyl: 0000, Head: 0, Sec: 00
	55=Reserved	Cyl: 0000, Head: 0, Sec: 00
	56=Reserved	Cyl: 0000, Head: 0, Sec: 00
	57=Reserved	Cyl: 0000, Head: 0, Sec: 00
	58=Reserved	Cyl: 0000, Head: 0, Sec: 00
	59=Reserved	Cyl: 0000, Head: 0, Sec: 00
	5A=Reserved	Cyl: 0000, Head: 0, Sec: 00
	5B=Reserved	Cyl: 0000, Head: 0, Sec: 00
	5C=Reserved	Cyl: 0000, Head: 0, Sec: 00
	5D=Reserved	Cyl: 0000, Head: 0, Sec: 00
	5E=Reserved	Cyl: 0000, Head: 0, Sec: 00
	5F=Reserved	Cyl: 0000, Head: 0, Sec: 00
	60=Read FPDMA Queued	Cyl: 0000, Head: 0, Sec: 00
	61=Write FPDMA Queued	Cyl: 0000, Head: 0, Sec: 00
	62=Reserved	Cyl: 0000, Head: 0, Sec: 00

63=Reserved	Cyl: 0000, Head: 0, Sec: 00	
64=Reserved	Cyl: 0000, Head: 0, Sec: 00	
65=Reserved	Cyl: 0000, Head: 0, Sec: 00	
66=Reserved	Cyl: 0000, Head: 0, Sec: 00	
67=SEP_ATTN	Cyl: 0000, Head: 0, Sec: 00	
68=Reserved	Cyl: 0000, Head: 0, Sec: 00	
69=Reserved	Cyl: 0000, Head: 0, Sec: 00	
6A=Reserved	Cyl: 0000, Head: 0, Sec: 00	
6B=Reserved	Cyl: 0000, Head: 0, Sec: 00	
6C=Reserved	Cyl: 0000, Head: 0, Sec: 00	
6D=Reserved	Cyl: 0000, Head: 0, Sec: 00	
6E=Reserved	Cyl: 0000, Head: 0, Sec: 00	
6F=Reserved	Cyl: 0000, Head: 0, Sec: 00	
70=SEEK	Cyl: 0000, Head: 0, Sec: 00	
71=SEEK	Cyl: 0000, Head: 0, Sec: 00	
72=SEEK	Cyl: 0000, Head: 0, Sec: 00	
73=SEEK	Cyl: 0000, Head: 0, Sec: 00	
74=SEEK	Cyl: 0000, Head: 0, Sec: 00	
75=SEEK	Cyl: 0000, Head: 0, Sec: 00	
76=SEEK	Cyl: 0000, Head: 0, Sec: 00	
77=SEEK	Cyl: 0000, Head: 0, Sec: 00	
78=SEEK	Cyl: 0000, Head: 0, Sec: 00	
79=SEEK	Cyl: 0000, Head: 0, Sec: 00	
7A=SEEK	Cyl: 0000, Head: 0, Sec: 00	
7B=SEEK	Cyl: 0000, Head: 0, Sec: 00	
7C=SEEK	Cyl: 0000, Head: 0, Sec: 00	
7D=SEEK	Cyl: 0000, Head: 0, Sec: 00	
7E=SEEK	Cyl: 0000, Head: 0, Sec: 00	
7F=SEEK	Cyl: 0000, Head: 0, Sec: 00	
80=Reserved	Cyl: 0000, Head: 0, Sec: 00	
81=Reserved	Cyl: 0000, Head: 0, Sec: 00	
82=Reserved	Cyl: 0000, Head: 0, Sec: 00	
83=Reserved	Cyl: 0000, Head: 0, Sec: 00	
84=Reserved	Cyl: 0000, Head: 0, Sec: 00	
85=Reserved	Cyl: 0000, Head: 0, Sec: 00	
86=Reserved	Cyl: 0000, Head: 0, Sec: 00	
87=CFA TRNSLT SCTR	LBA=0000000	
88=Reserved	Cyl: 0000, Head: 0, Sec: 00	
89=Reserved	Cyl: 0000, Head: 0, Sec: 00	
8A=Reserved	Cyl: 0000, Head: 0, Sec: 00	
8B=Reserved	Cyl: 0000, Head: 0, Sec: 00	
8C=Reserved	Cyl: 0000, Head: 0, Sec: 00	
8D=Reserved	Cyl: 0000, Head: 0, Sec: 00	
8E=Reserved	Cyl: 0000, Head: 0, Sec: 00	
8F=Reserved	Cyl: 0000, Head: 0, Sec: 00	
90=EXEC DRIVE DIAG	Cyl: 0000, Head: 0, Sec: 00	

93=Reserved	Cyl: 0000, Head: 0, Sec: 00
94=STANDBY IMMEDIA	Cyl: 0000, Head: 0, Sec: 00
95=IDLE IMMEDIATE	Cyl: 0000, Head: 0, Sec: 00
96=STANDBY	Cyl: 0000, Head: 0, Sec: 00
97=IDLE	Cyl: 0000, Head: 0, Sec: 00
98=CHECK POWER MOD	Cyl: 0000, Head: 0, Sec: 00
99=SLEEP	Cyl: 0000, Head: 0, Sec: 00
9A=Reserved	Cyl: 0000, Head: 0, Sec: 00
9B=Reserved	Cyl: 0000, Head: 0, Sec: 00
9C=Reserved	Cyl: 0000, Head: 0, Sec: 00
9D=Reserved	Cyl: 0000, Head: 0, Sec: 00
9E=Reserved	Cyl: 0000, Head: 0, Sec: 00
9F=Reserved	Cyl: 0000, Head: 0, Sec: 00
A1=ATAPI ID DRIVE	Cyl: 0000, Head: 0, Sec: 00
A2=ATAPI SERVICE	Cyl: 0000, Head: 0, Sec: 00
A3=Reserved	Cyl: 0000, Head: 0, Sec: 00
A4=Reserved	Cyl: 0000, Head: 0, Sec: 00
A5=Reserved	Cyl: 0000, Head: 0, Sec: 00
A6=Reserved	Cyl: 0000, Head: 0, Sec: 00
A7=Reserved	Cyl: 0000, Head: 0, Sec: 00
A8=Reserved	Cyl: 0000, Head: 0, Sec: 00
A9=Reserved	Cyl: 0000, Head: 0, Sec: 00
AA=Reserved	Cyl: 0000, Head: 0, Sec: 00
AB=Reserved	Cyl: 0000, Head: 0, Sec: 00
AC=Reserved	Cyl: 0000, Head: 0, Sec: 00
AD=Reserved	Cyl: 0000, Head: 0, Sec: 00
AE=Reserved	Cyl: 0000, Head: 0, Sec: 00
AF=Reserved	Cyl: 0000, Head: 0, Sec: 00
B0=SMART D9=Smart Disable Operation	Cyl: 0000, Head: 0, Sec: 00
B0=SMART DA=Smart Return Stats	Cyl: 0000, Head: 0, Sec: 00
B0=SMART D2=Smart Enable/Disable AT	Cyl: 0000, Head: 0, Sec: 00
B0=SMART D8=Smart Enable Operation	Cyl: 0000, Head: 0, Sec: 00
B0=SMART D4=Smart Execute Offline	Cyl: 0000, Head: 0, Sec: 00
B1=Device Config	Cyl: 0000, Head: 0, Sec: 00
B1=Device Config	Cyl: 0000, Head: 0, Sec: 00
B2=Reserved	Cyl: 0000, Head: 0, Sec: 00
B3=Reserved	Cyl: 0000, Head: 0, Sec: 00
B4=Reserved	Cyl: 0000, Head: 0, Sec: 00
B5=Reserved	Cyl: 0000, Head: 0, Sec: 00
B6=Reserved	Cyl: 0000, Head: 0, Sec: 00
B7=Reserved	Cyl: 0000, Head: 0, Sec: 00

B8=Reserved	Cyl: 0000, Head: 0, Sec: 00	
B9=Reserved	Cyl: 0000, Head: 0, Sec: 00	
BA=Reserved	Cyl: 0000, Head: 0, Sec: 00	
BB=Reserved	Cyl: 0000, Head: 0, Sec: 00	
BC=Reserved	Cyl: 0000, Head: 0, Sec: 00	
BD=Reserved	Cyl: 0000, Head: 0, Sec: 00	
BE=Reserved	Cyl: 0000, Head: 0, Sec: 00	
BF=Reserved	Cyl: 0000, Head: 0, Sec: 00	
C1=Reserved	Cyl: 0000, Head: 0, Sec: 00	
C2=Reserved	Cyl: 0000, Head: 0, Sec: 00	
C3=Reserved	Cyl: 0000, Head: 0, Sec: 00	
C6=SET MULTPLE MOD	Cyl: 0000, Head: 0, Sec: 00	
CF=Reserved	Cyl: 0000, Head: 0, Sec: 00	
D0=Reserved	Cyl: 0000, Head: 0, Sec: 00	
D1=CHK MD Card Type	Cyl: 0000, Head: 0, Sec: 00	
D2=Reserved	Cyl: 0000, Head: 0, Sec: 00	
D3=Reserved	Cyl: 0000, Head: 0, Sec: 00	
D4=Reserved	Cyl: 0000, Head: 0, Sec: 00	
D5=Reserved	Cyl: 0000, Head: 0, Sec: 00	
D6=Reserved	Cyl: 0000, Head: 0, Sec: 00	
D7=Reserved	Cyl: 0000, Head: 0, Sec: 00	
D8=Reserved	Cyl: 0000, Head: 0, Sec: 00	
D9=Reserved	Cyl: 0000, Head: 0, Sec: 00	
DA=Get Media Sts	Cyl: 0000, Head: 0, Sec: 00	
DB=ACK MEDIA CHG	Cyl: 0000, Head: 0, Sec: 00	
DC=BOOT POST-BOOT	Cyl: 0000, Head: 0, Sec: 00	
DD=BOOT PRE-BOOT	Cyl: 0000, Head: 0, Sec: 00	
DE=MEDIA LOCK	Cyl: 0000, Head: 0, Sec: 00	
DF=MEDIA UNLOCK	Cyl: 0000, Head: 0, Sec: 00	
E0=STANDBY IMMEDIA	Cyl: 0000, Head: 0, Sec: 00	
E1=IDLE IMMEDIATE	Cyl: 0000, Head: 0, Sec: 00	
E2=STANDBY	Cyl: 0000, Head: 0, Sec: 00	
E3=IDLE	Cyl: 0000, Head: 0, Sec: 00	
E5=CHECK POWER MOD	Cyl: 0000, Head: 0, Sec: 00	
E6=SLEEP	Cyl: 0000, Head: 0, Sec: 00	
EB=Reserved	Cyl: 0000, Head: 0, Sec: 00	
EC=IDENTIFY DRIVE	Cyl: 0000, Head: 0, Sec: 00	
ED=MEDIA EJECT	Cyl: 0000, Head: 0, Sec: 00	
EE=IDENT DEVICE DM	Cyl: 0000, Head: 0, Sec: 00	
EF=SET FEATURES 00=Unknown	Cyl: 0000, Head: 0, Sec: 00	
F0=Reserved	Cyl: 0000, Head: 0, Sec: 00	
F2=SECURITY UNLOCK	Cyl: 0000, Head: 0, Sec: 00	
F5=SECURITY FREEZE	Cyl: 0000, Head: 0, Sec: 00	
F6=SECUR DSABL PAS	Cyl: 0000, Head: 0, Sec: 00	
F7=Reserved	Cyl: 0000, Head: 0, Sec: 00	

	FA=Reserved	Cyl: 0000, Head: 0, Sec: 00
	FB=Reserved	Cyl: 0000, Head: 0, Sec: 00
	FC=Reserved	Cyl: 0000, Head: 0, Sec: 00
	FD=Reserved	Cyl: 0000, Head: 0, Sec: 00
	FE=Reserved	Cyl: 0000, Head: 0, Sec: 00
	FF=Reserved	Cyl: 0000, Head: 0, Sec: 00

208 commands sent, 204 commands allowed

Results:	Assertion	Expected Result	Actual Result
	AM-01	Modifying commands blocked	Modifying commands blocked
	AM-05	HWB behavior recorded	HWB behavior recorded
Analysis:	Expected results achieved		

Test Case HWB-01 Variation 01-r ICS ImageMasster DriveLock IDE FW v17	
Case Summary:	HWB-01 Identify commands blocked by the HWB.
Assertions Tested:	HWB-AM-01 The HWB shall not transmit any modifying category operation to the protected storage device. HWB-AM-05 The action that an HWB device takes for any commands not assigned to the modifying, read, or information categories is defined by the vendor.
Tester Name:	kbr
Test Date:	run start Mon Aug 29 11:23:42 2005 run finish Mon Aug 29 11:25:48 2005
Test Configuration:	HOST: freddy HostToBlocker Monitor: dale HostToBlocker PA: aa00155 HostToBlocker Interface: IDE BlockerToDrive Monitor: chip BlockerToDrive PA: aa00111 BlockerToDrive Interface: IDE Run Environment: DOS
Drives:	Protected drive: bf bf is a WDC WD2500JB-00GVA0 serial # WD-WCAL73854148 with 488397168 sectors
Blocker Input:	Commands Sent to Blocker

Command	LBA/CHS
20=READ W/ RETRY	LBA=0002000
21=READ W/O RETRY	LBA=0002100
22=READ/L W/ RETRY	LBA=0002200
23=READ/L W/O RETR	LBA=0002300
24=READ SECTOR EXT	LBA=000000002400
25=READ DMA EXT	LBA=000000002500
26=RD DMA QUE EXT	LBA=000000002600

	27=RD MAX ADR EXT	LBA=000000002700
	29=READ MULTI EXT	LBA=0002900
	2A=READ STREAM DMA	LBA=000000002A00
	2B=READ STREAM PIO	LBA=000000002B00
	2F=READ LOG EXT	LBA=000000002F00
	40=READ/V W/ RETRY	LBA=0004000
	41=READ/V W/O RETR	LBA=0004100
	42=READ/V W/ EXT	LBA=000000004200
	B0=SMART D0=SMART READ DATA	Cyl: 0000, Head: 0, Sec: 00
	B0=SMART D5=Smart Read Log	Cyl: 0000, Head: 0, Sec: 00
	C4=READ MULTIPLE	LBA=000C400
	C7=READ DMA QUEUED	LBA=000C700
	C8=Read DMA	LBA=000C800
	C9=RD DMA W/O RETR	LBA=000C900
	E4=READ BUFFER	Cyl: 00E4, Head: 0, Sec: 00
	F8=RD NATV MAX ADD	LBA=000F800

23 commands sent

Blocker Output:	Commands Allowed by Blocker	
	Command	LBA/CHS
	20=READ W/ RETRY	LBA=0002000
	21=READ W/O RETRY	LBA=0002100
	22=READ/L W/ RETRY	LBA=0002200
	23=READ/L W/O RETR	LBA=0002300
	24=READ SECTOR EXT	LBA=000000002400
	25=READ DMA EXT	LBA=000000002500
	26=RD DMA QUE EXT	LBA=000000002600
	27=RD MAX ADR EXT	LBA=000000002700
	29=READ MULTI EXT	LBA=0002900
	2A=READ STREAM DMA	LBA=000000002A00
	2B=READ STREAM PIO	LBA=000000002B00
	2F=READ LOG EXT	LBA=000000002F00
	40=READ/V W/ RETRY	LBA=0004000
	41=READ/V W/O RETR	LBA=0004100
	42=READ/V W/ EXT	LBA=000000004200
	B0=SMART D0=SMART READ DATA	Cyl: 0000, Head: 0, Sec: 00
	B0=SMART D5=Smart Read Log	Cyl: 0000, Head: 0, Sec: 00
	C4=READ MULTIPLE	LBA=000C400
	C7=READ DMA QUEUED	LBA=000C700
	C8=Read DMA	LBA=000C800
	C9=RD DMA W/O RETR	LBA=000C900

	E4=READ BUFFER	Cyl: 00E4, Head: 0, Sec: 00
	F8=RD NATV MAX ADD	LBA=000F800
	23 commands sent, 23 commands allowed	

	Assertion	Expected Result	Actual Result
Results:	AM-01	Modifying commands blocked	Modifying commands blocked
	AM-05	HWB behavior recorded	HWB behavior recorded
Analysis:	Expected results achieved		

Test Case HWB-01 Variation 01-w ICS ImageMasster DriveLock IDE FW v17	
Case Summary:	HWB-01 Identify commands blocked by the HWB.
Assertions Tested:	HWB-AM-01 The HWB shall not transmit any modifying category operation to the protected storage device. HWB-AM-05 The action that an HWB device takes for any commands not assigned to the modifying, read, or information categories is defined by the vendor.
Tester Name:	kbr
Test Date:	run start Mon Aug 29 11:17:16 2005 run finish Mon Aug 29 11:20:42 2005
Test Configuration:	HOST: freddy HostToBlocker Monitor: dale HostToBlocker PA: aa00155 HostToBlocker Interface: IDE BlockerToDrive Monitor: chip BlockerToDrive PA: aa00111 BlockerToDrive Interface: IDE Run Environment: DOS
Drives:	Protected drive: bf bf is a WDC WD2500JB-00GVA0 serial # WD-WCAL73854148 with 488397168 sectors
Blocker Input:	Commands Sent to Blocker

Command	LBA/CHS
30=WRITE W/ RETRY	LBA=0000000
31=WRITE W/O RETRY	LBA=0000000
32=WRITE/L W/ RETR	LBA=0000000
33=WRITE/L W/O RTR	LBA=0000000
34=WRITE SECTOR EXT	LBA=000000000000
35=WRITE DMA EXT	LBA=000000000000
36=WR DMA QUE EXT	LBA=000000000000
38=CFA WRT SEC W/O	LBA=0000000
39=WRITE MULTI EXT	LBA=000000000000
3A=WRITE STREAM DMA	LBA=000000000000
3B=WRITE STREAM PIO	LBA=000000000000

	3D=Reserved	LBA=0000000
	3E=Reserved	LBA=0000000
	3F=WRITE LOG EXT	LBA=000000000000
	Pkt=	
	B0=SMART D6=Smart Write Log	Cyl: 0000, Head: 0, Sec: 00
	C0=CFA ERASE SECTR	LBA=0000000
	C5=WRITE MULTIPLE	LBA=0000000
	CA=Write DMA	LBA=0000000
	CB=WRT DMA W/O RTR	LBA=0000000
	CC=WRITE DMA QUEUE	LBA=0000000
	CD=CFA WRT MULT W/	LBA=0000000
	CE=Reserved	LBA=0000000
	E7=FLUSH CACHE	Cyl: 0000, Head: 0, Sec: 00
	E8=WRITE BUFFER	Cyl: 0000, Head: 0, Sec: 00
	E9=WRITE SAME	Cyl: 0000, Head: 0, Sec: 00
	EA=FLUSH CACHE EXT	LBA=000000000000
	F3=SECUR ERASE PRE	Cyl: 0000, Head: 0, Sec: 00
	F4=SECUR ERASE UNI	Cyl: 0000, Head: 0, Sec: 00

29 commands sent

Blocker Output:	Commands Allowed by Blocker	
	Command	LBA/CHS
	38=CFA WRT SEC W/O	LBA=0000000
	3D=Reserved	LBA=0000000
	3E=Reserved	LBA=0000000
	3F=WRITE LOG EXT	LBA=000000000000
	Pkt=	
	B0=SMART D6=Smart Write Log	Cyl: 0000, Head: 0, Sec: 00
	C0=CFA ERASE SECTR	LBA=0000000
	CD=CFA WRT MULT W/	LBA=0000000
	CE=Reserved	LBA=0000000
	E8=WRITE BUFFER	Cyl: 0000, Head: 0, Sec: 00

29 commands sent, 10 commands allowed

Results:	Assertion	Expected Result	Actual Result
	AM-01	Modifying commands blocked	Modifying commands blocked
	AM-05	HWB behavior recorded	HWB behavior recorded

Analysis:	Expected results achieved

Test Case HWB-01 Variation 01-x ICS ImageMasster DriveLock IDE FW v17	
Case Summary:	HWB-01 Identify commands blocked by the HWB.
Assertions Tested:	HWB-AM-01 The HWB shall not transmit any modifying category operation to the protected storage device. HWB-AM-05 The action that an HWB device takes for any commands not assigned to the modifying, read, or information categories is defined by the vendor.
Tester Name:	kbr
Test Date:	run start Thu Sep 1 14:32:43 2005
Test Configuration:	HOST: freddy HostToBlocker Monitor: dale HostToBlocker PA: aa00155 HostToBlocker Interface: IDE BlockerToDrive Monitor: chip BlockerToDrive PA: aa00111 BlockerToDrive Interface: IDE Run Environment: DOS
Drives:	Protected drive: xx xx is a MAXTOR 88400DB with 16408224 sectors
Blocker Input:	Commands Sent to Blocker
Blocker Output:	Commands Allowed by Blocker
Results:	
Analysis:	Expected results achieved

Blocker Input — Commands Sent to Blocker:

Command	LBA/CHS
50=FORMAT TRACK	Cyl: 0000, Head: 0, Sec: 00
91=INIT DRV PARAMS	Cyl: 0000, Head: 0, Sec: 00
92=DOWNLD MICROCOD	Cyl: 0000, Head: 0, Sec: 00
F1=SECUR SET PASSW	Cyl: 0000, Head: 0, Sec: 00

4 commands sent

Blocker Output — Commands Allowed by Blocker:

Command	LBA/CHS
50=FORMAT TRACK	Cyl: 0000, Head: 0, Sec: 00
91=INIT DRV PARAMS	Cyl: 0000, Head: 0, Sec: 00

4 commands sent, 2 commands allowed

Results:

Assertion	Expected Result	Actual Result
AM-01	Modifying commands blocked	Modifying commands blocked
AM-05	HWB behavior recorded	HWB behavior recorded

Test Case HWB-03 Variation hwb-03-boot ICS ImageMasster DriveLock IDE FW v17	
Case Summary:	HWB-03 Identify commands blocked by the HWB while attempting to

	modify a protected drive with forensic tools.
Assertions Tested:	HWB-AM-01 The HWB shall not transmit any modifying category operation to the protected storage device. HWB-AM-05 The action that an HWB device takes for any commands not assigned to the modifying, read, or information categories is defined by the vendor.
Tester Name:	kbr
Test Date:	run start Thu Sep 1 11:19:13 2005 run finish Thu Sep 1 11:20:22 2005
Test Configuration:	HOST: beta5 HostToBlocker Monitor: dale HostToBlocker PA: aa00155 HostToBlocker Interface: IDE BlockerToDrive Monitor: chip BlockerToDrive PA: aa00111 BlockerToDrive Interface: IDE Run Environment: W2k
Drives:	Protected drive: 7c 7c is a MAXTOR 6L040J2 serial # 662201137769 with 78177792 sectors
Blocker Input:	Commands Sent to Blocker
Blocker Output:	Commands Allowed by Blocker

Blocker Input — Commands Sent to Blocker:

Count	Commands
21	20=READ W/ RETRY
1	90=EXEC DRIVE DIAG
91	C4=READ MULTIPLE
1	C6=SET MULTPLE MOD
919	C8=Read DMA
1	E3=IDLE
1	EC=IDENTIFY DRIVE
2	EF=SET FEATURES 03=Set Transfer Mode (Use Sec Cnt)

Blocker Output — Commands Allowed by Blocker:

Count	Commands
21	20=READ W/ RETRY
1	90=EXEC DRIVE DIAG
91	C4=READ MULTIPLE
1	C6=SET MULTPLE MOD
919	C8=Read DMA
1	E3=IDLE
1	EC=IDENTIFY DRIVE
2	EF=SET FEATURES 03=Set Transfer Mode (Use Sec Cnt)

Results:	Assertion	Expected Result	Actual Result
	AM-01	Modifying commands blocked	Modifying commands blocked
	AM-05	HWB behavior recorded	HWB behavior recorded
Analysis:	Expected results achieved		

Test Case HWB-03 Variation hwb-03-img ICS ImageMasster DriveLock IDE FW v17	
Case Summary:	HWB-03 Identify commands blocked by the HWB while attempting to modify a protected drive with forensic tools.
Assertions Tested:	HWB-AM-01 The HWB shall not transmit any modifying category operation to the protected storage device. HWB-AM-05 The action that an HWB device takes for any commands not assigned to the modifying, read, or information categories is defined by the vendor.
Tester Name:	kbr
Test Date:	run start Thu Sep 1 11:52:44 2005 run finish Thu Sep 1 11:54:59 2005
Test Configuration:	HOST: freddy HostToBlocker Monitor: dale HostToBlocker PA: aa00155 HostToBlocker Interface: IDE BlockerToDrive Monitor: chip BlockerToDrive PA: aa00111 BlockerToDrive Interface: IDE Run Environment: IX
Drives:	Protected drive: 74 74 is a IC35L040AVER07-0 serial # SXPTXHQ6113 with 80418240 sectors
Blocker Input:	Commands Sent to Blocker

Count	Commands
12	C8=Read DMA
270	CA=Write DMA

Blocker Output:	Commands Allowed by Blocker

Count	Commands
12	C8=Read DMA

Results:	Assertion	Expected Result	Actual Result
	AM-01	Modifying commands blocked	Modifying commands blocked
	AM-05	HWB behavior recorded	HWB behavior recorded
Analysis:	Expected results achieved		

Test Case HWB-06 Variation hwb-06-en ICS ImageMasster DriveLock IDE FW v17	
Case Summary:	HWB-06 Identify read and information commands used by forensic tools and allowed by the HWB.

Assertions Tested:	HWB-AM-02 If the host sends a read category operation to the HWB and no error is returned from the protected storage device to the HWB, then the data addressed by the original read operation is returned to the host.
	HWB-AM-03 If the host sends an information category operation to the HWB and if there is no error on the protected storage device, then any returned access-significant information is returned to the host without modification.
	HWB-AM-05 The action that an HWB device takes for any commands not assigned to the modifying, read, or information categories is defined by the vendor.
Tester Name:	kbr
Test Date:	run start Fri Sep 2 10:54:14 2005
	run finish Fri Sep 2 11:00:23 2005
Test Configuration:	HOST: freddy
	HostToBlocker Monitor: dale
	HostToBlocker PA: aa00155
	HostToBlocker Interface: IDE
	BlockerToDrive Monitor: chip
	BlockerToDrive PA: aa00111
	BlockerToDrive Interface: IDE
	Run Environment: DOES
Drives:	Protected drive: a8
	a8 is a WDC WD200BB-00AUA1 serial # WD-WMA6Y3401179 with 39102336 sectors

Blocker Input: Commands Sent to Blocker

Count	Commands
252	20=READ W/ RETRY

Blocker Output: Commands Allowed by Blocker

Count	Commands
252	20=READ W/ RETRY

Results:

Assertion	Expected Result	Actual Result
AM-02	Read commands allowed	Read commands allowed
AM-03	Access Significant Information unaltered	Access Significant Information unaltered
AM-05	HWB behavior recorded	HWB behavior recorded

Analysis: Expected results achieved

Test Case HWB-06 Variation hwb-06-ix ICS ImageMasster DriveLock IDE FW v17	
Case Summary:	HWB-06 Identify read and information commands used by forensic tools and allowed by the HWB.
Assertions Tested:	HWB-AM-02 If the host sends a read category operation to the HWB and no error is returned from the protected storage device to the HWB, then the data

addressed by the original read operation is returned to the host.

HWB-AM-03 If the host sends an information category operation to the HWB and if there is no error on the protected storage device, then any returned access-significant information is returned to the host without modification.

HWB-AM-05 The action that an HWB device takes for any commands not assigned to the modifying, read, or information categories is defined by the vendor.

Tester Name:	kbr
Test Date:	run start Fri Sep 2 11:26:08 2005 run finish Fri Sep 2 11:29:07 2005
Test Configuration:	HOST: freddy HostToBlocker Monitor: dale HostToBlocker PA: aa00155 HostToBlocker Interface: IDE BlockerToDrive Monitor: chip BlockerToDrive PA: aa00111 BlockerToDrive Interface: IDE Run Environment: IX
Drives:	Protected drive: bf bf is a WDC WD2500JB-00GVA0 serial # WD-WCAL73854148 with 488397168 sectors

Blocker Input:	Commands Sent to Blocker	
	Count	Commands
	132	25=READ DMA EXT

Blocker Output:	Commands Allowed by Blocker	
	Count	Commands
	132	25=READ DMA EXT

Results:	Assertion	Expected Result	Actual Result
	AM-02	Read commands allowed	Read commands allowed
	AM-03	Access Significant Information unaltered	Access Significant Information unaltered
	AM-05	HWB behavior recorded	HWB behavior recorded
Analysis:	Expected results achieved		

Test Case HWB-08 Variation hwb-08 ICS ImageMasster DriveLock IDE FW v17	
Case Summary:	HWB-08 Identify access significant information unmodified by the HWB.
Assertions Tested:	HWB-AM-03 If the host sends an information category operation to the HWB and if there is no error on the protected storage device, then any returned access-significant information is returned to the host without modification.

Tester Name:	kbr
Test Date:	run start Wed Aug 31 09:34:20 2005
	run finish Wed Aug 31 09:35:32 2005
Test Configuration:	HOST: freddy
	HostToBlocker Monitor: none
	HostToBlocker PA: none
	HostToBlocker Interface: IDE
	BlockerToDrive Monitor: none
	BlockerToDrive PA: none
	BlockerToDrive Interface: IDE
	Run Environment: DOS
Drives:	Protected drive: bf
	bf is a WDC WD2500JB-00GVA0 serial # WD-WCAL73854148 with 488397168 sectors
Blocker Output:	cmd: z:\ss\PARTAB.EXE hwb-08 freddy 80 /all
	488397168 sectors

Results:	Assertion	Expected Result	Actual Result
	AM-03	Access Significant Information unaltered	Access Significant Information unaltered

Analysis:	Expected results achieved

Test Case HWB-09 Variation hwb-09 ICS ImageMasster DriveLock IDE FW v17	
Case Summary:	HWB-09 Determine if an error on the protected drive is returned to the host.
Assertions Tested:	HWB-AM-04 If the host sends an operation to the HWB and if the operation results in an unresolved error on the protected storage device, then the HWB shall return an error status code to the host.
Tester Name:	kbr
Test Date:	run start Thu Sep 1 14:44:33 2005
	run finish Thu Sep 1 14:46:56 2005
Test Configuration:	HOST: freddy
	HostToBlocker Monitor: none
	HostToBlocker PA: none
	HostToBlocker Interface: IDE
	BlockerToDrive Monitor: none
	BlockerToDrive PA: none
	BlockerToDrive Interface: IDE
	Run Environment: DOS
Drives:	Protected drive: a8
	a8 is a WDC WD200BB-00AUA1 serial # WD-WMA6Y3401179 with 39102336 sectors
Blocker Output:	39102336 total number of sectors reported via interrupt 13 from the BIOS
	cmd: Z:\SS\DISKCHG.EXE hwb-09 freddy 80 /read 49102336 0 512
	Disk addr lba 49102336 C/H/S 48712/10/11 offset 0
	Disk read error 0x04 at sector 48712/10/11

Results:	Assertion	Expected Result	Actual Result	
	AM-04	Error code returned AM-04	Error code returned	
Analysis:	Expected results achieved			

About the National Institute of Justice

NIJ is the research, development, and evaluation agency of the U.S. Department of Justice. NIJ's mission is to advance scientific research, development, and evaluation to enhance the administration of justice and public safety. NIJ's principal authorities are derived from the Omnibus Crime Control and Safe Streets Act of 1968, as amended (see 42 U.S.C. §§ 3721–3723).

The NIJ Director is appointed by the President and confirmed by the Senate. The Director establishes the Institute's objectives, guided by the priorities of the Office of Justice Programs, the U.S. Department of Justice, and the needs of the field. The Institute actively solicits the views of criminal justice and other professionals and researchers to inform its search for the knowledge and tools to guide policy and practice.

Strategic Goals

NIJ has seven strategic goals grouped into three categories:

Creating relevant knowledge and tools

1. Partner with State and local practitioners and policymakers to identify social science research and technology needs.
2. Create scientific, relevant, and reliable knowledge—with a particular emphasis on terrorism, violent crime, drugs and crime, cost-effectiveness, and community-based efforts—to enhance the administration of justice and public safety.
3. Develop affordable and effective tools and technologies to enhance the administration of justice and public safety.

Dissemination

4. Disseminate relevant knowledge and information to practitioners and policymakers in an understandable, timely, and concise manner.
5. Act as an honest broker to identify the information, tools, and technologies that respond to the needs of stakeholders.

Agency management

6. Practice fairness and openness in the research and development process.
7. Ensure professionalism, excellence, accountability, cost-effectiveness, and integrity in the management and conduct of NIJ activities and programs.

Program Areas

In addressing these strategic challenges, the Institute is involved in the following program areas: crime control and prevention, including policing; drugs and crime; justice systems and offender behavior, including corrections; violence and victimization; communications and information technologies; critical incident response; investigative and forensic sciences, including DNA; less-than-lethal technologies; officer protection; education and training technologies; testing and standards; technology assistance to law enforcement and corrections agencies; field testing of promising programs; and international crime control.

In addition to sponsoring research and development and technology assistance, NIJ evaluates programs, policies, and technologies. NIJ communicates its research and evaluation findings through conferences and print and electronic media.

To find out more about the National Institute of Justice, please visit:

http://www.ojp.usdoj.gov/nij

or contact:

National Criminal Justice
 Reference Service
P.O. Box 6000
Rockville, MD 20849–6000
800–851–3420
e-mail: *askncjrs@ncjrs.org*